VOCAL SELECTIONS

THE GREATEST SHOWMAN - MUSIC FROM THE MOTION PICTURE SOUNDTRACK

ORIGINAL SONGS BY
BENJ PASEK & JUSTIN PAUL

ISBN 978-1-5400-2505-0

7777 W. BLUEMOUND RD. P.O. BOX 13819 MILWAUKEE, WI 53213

In Australia Contact:
Hal Leonard Australia Pty. Ltd.
4 Lentara Court
Cheltenham, Victoria, 3192 Australia
Email: ausadmin@halleonard.com.au

Visit Hal Leonard Online at
www.halleonard.com

THE GREATEST SHOW

Words and Music by BENJ PASEK,
JUSTIN PAUL and RYAN LEWIS

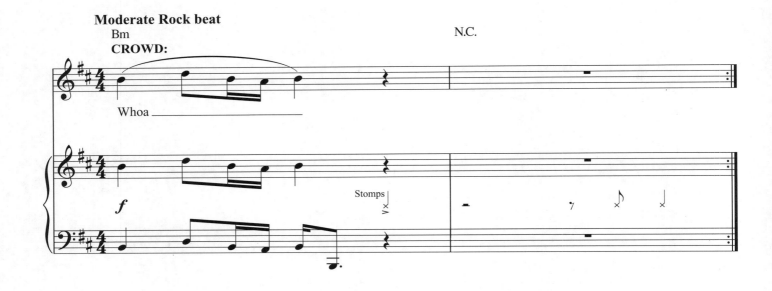

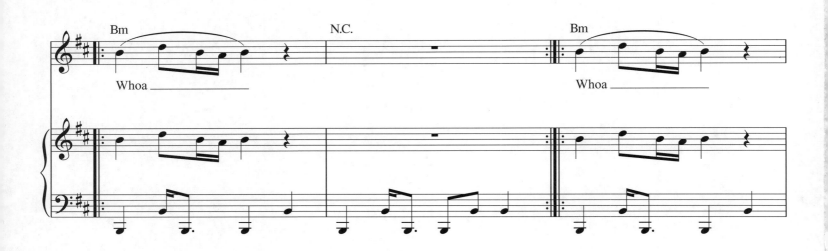

COME ALIVE

Words and Music by BENJ PASEK
and JUSTIN PAUL

18

A MILLION DREAMS

Words and Music by BENJ PASEK
and JUSTIN PAUL

* *Young Barnum written at pitch; Barnum written 8va.*

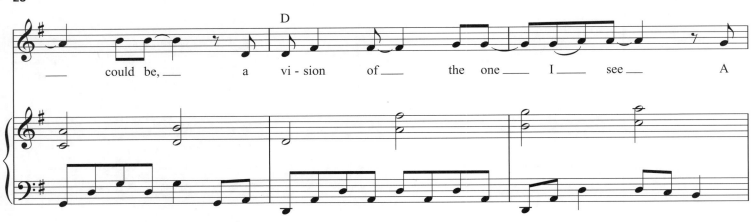

could be, ___ a vi - sion of ___ the one ___ I ___ see ___ A

mil - lion dreams ___ is all ___ it's gon - na take ___

Oh, a mil - lion dreams ___ for the world we're gon - na make

THE OTHER SIDE

Words and Music by BENJ PASEK
and JUSTIN PAUL

You're on-to some-thin' Real-ly, it's some-thin' But I live a-mong the swells, and

we don't pick up pea-nut shells I'll have to leave that up to you

D.S. al Coda

BARNUM: Now is this real-ly how __ you'd like to spend __ your days? Whis-
see the __ oth - er side

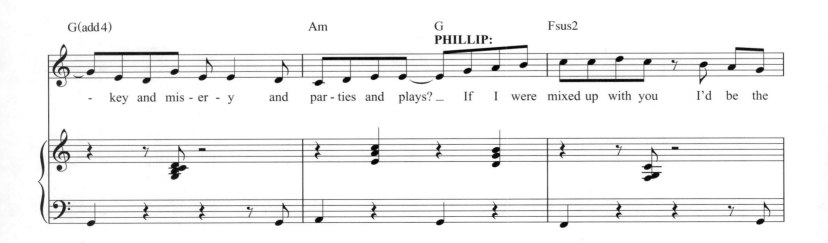

- key and mis - er - y and par-ties and plays? __ If I were mixed up with you I'd be the

PHILLIP:

seems worth tak - in' but I guess I'll leave that up to you

Tempo I

PHILLIP:

Well, it's in - trigu - ing, but to go ____ would cost me great - ly

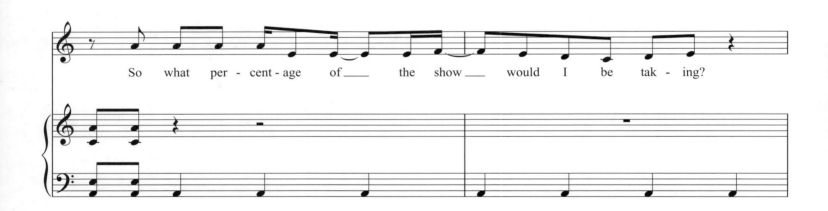

So what per - cent - age of ____ the show ____ would I be tak - ing?

BARNUM:

Well, fair e - nough, ____ you'd want a piece ____ of all ____ the ac - tion

44

NEVER ENOUGH

Words and Music by BENJ PASEK
and JUSTIN PAUL

48

THIS IS ME

Words and Music by BENJ PASEK
and JUSTIN PAUL

60

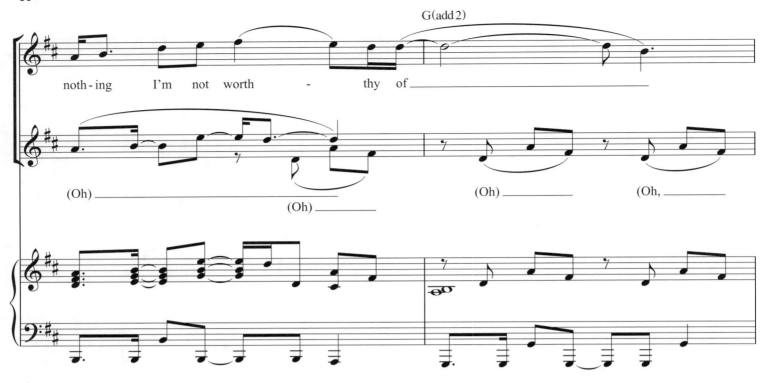

noth-ing I'm not worth - thy of _____

(Oh) _____ (Oh) _____ (Oh, _____

(Oh) _____

oh,   oh)   When the sharp - est words ___ wan-na cut me down _____

_____   I'm gon-na send a flood, ___ gon-na drown 'em out _____

REWRITE THE STARS

Words and Music by BENJ PASEK
and JUSTIN PAUL

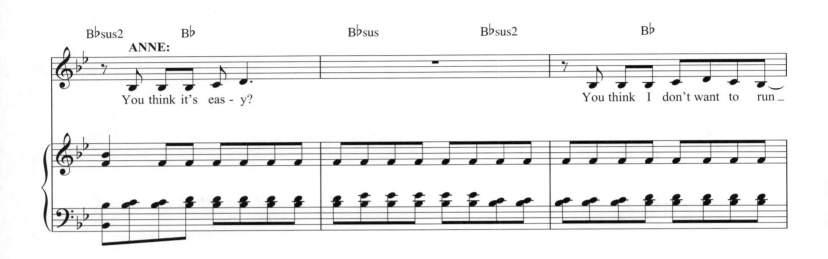

ANNE: You think it's eas-y? You think I don't want to run

to you? But there are moun-tains,

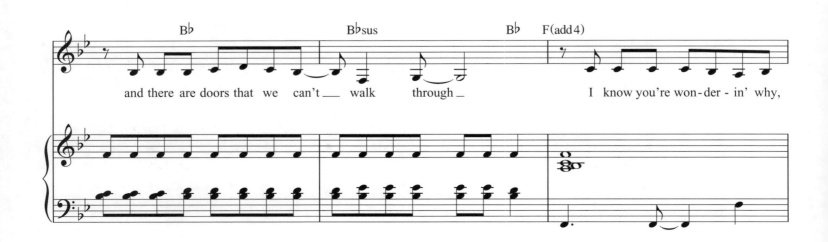

and there are doors that we can't walk through I know you're won-der-in' why,

TIGHTROPE

Words and Music by BENJ PASEK
and JUSTIN PAUL

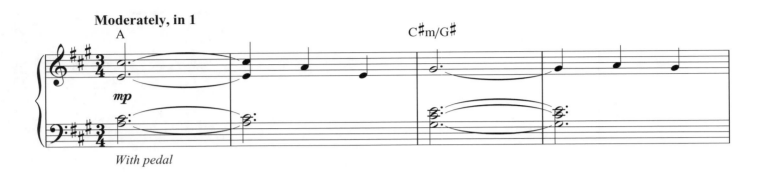

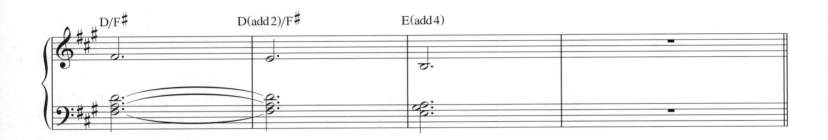

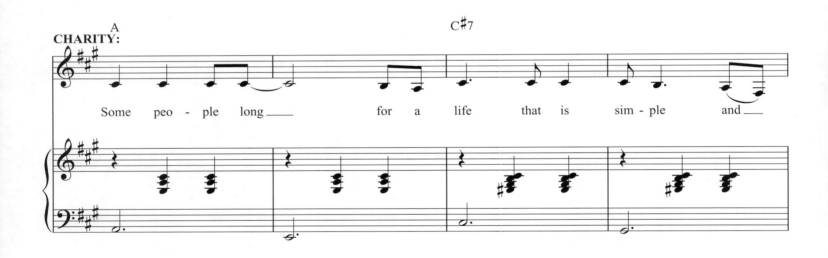

Some peo-ple long _____ for a life that is sim-ple and _____

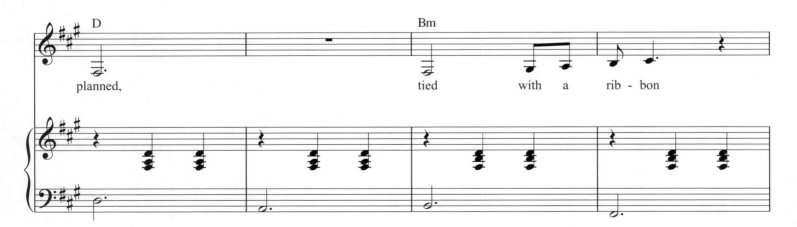

planned, tied with a rib-bon

74

FROM NOW ON

Words and Music by BENJ PASEK
and JUSTIN PAUL

*1st verse: Lead vocal written two octaves higher.

on _____ what's wait-ed 'til to-mor-row starts to-night, _____ to-

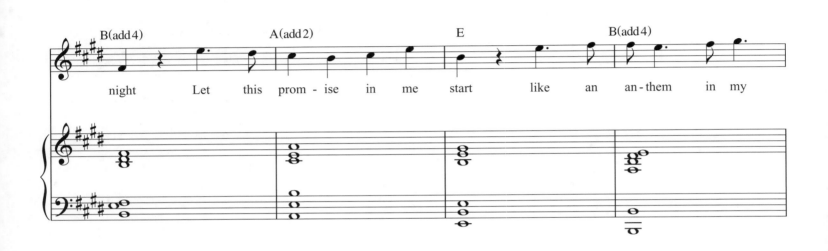

night _____ Let this prom-ise in me start like an an-them in my

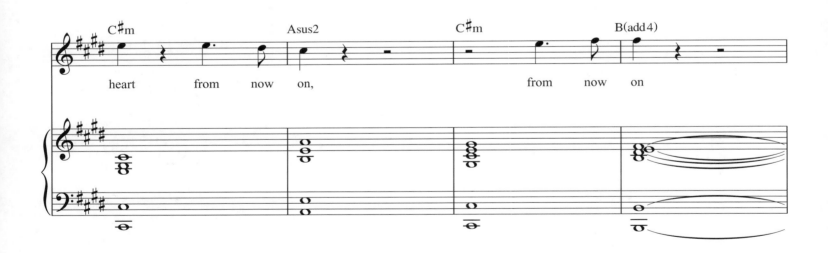

heart _____ from now on, _____ from now on

Moderately in 2

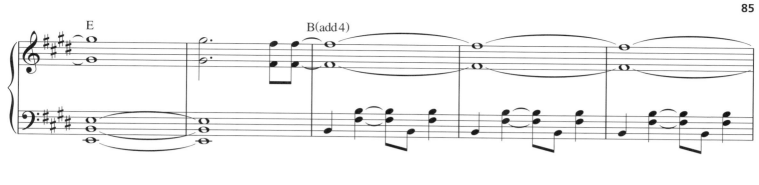

I drank cham - pagne with kings and queens, __ the

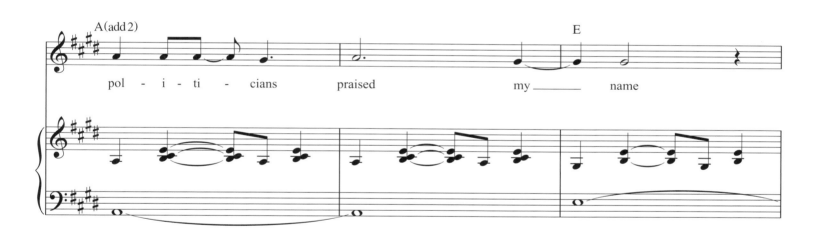

pol - i - ti - cians praised my ___ name

But those were __ some - one

Lead vocal written an octave higher.

else - 's dreams, the pit - falls of the man I ____ be -

____ came ____ For

years ____ and ____ years I chased their ____ cheers, ____ a

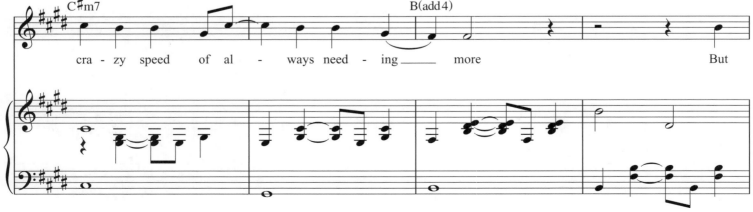

cra - zy speed of al - ways need - ing ____ more But

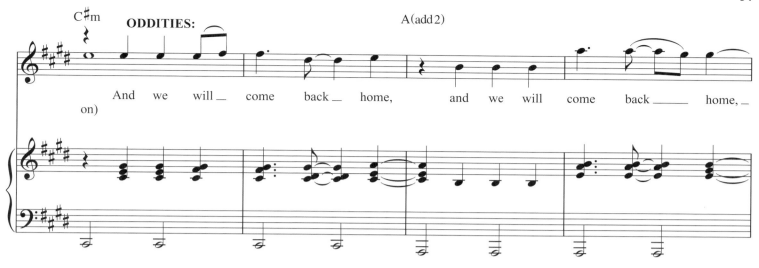

ODDITIES:

And we will come back home, and we will come back home,
(on)

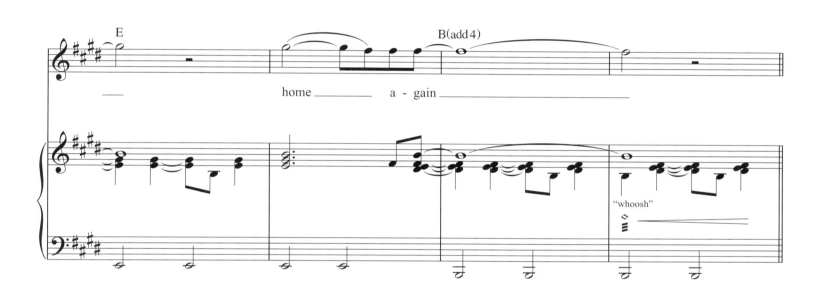

home a - gain

"whoosh"

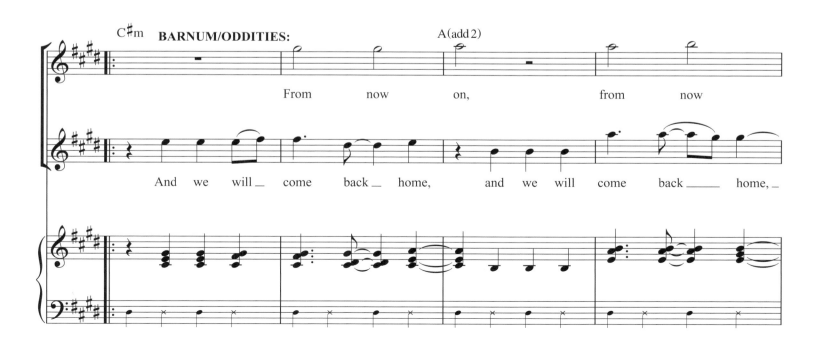

BARNUM/ODDITIES:

From now on, from now

And we will come back home, and we will come back home,

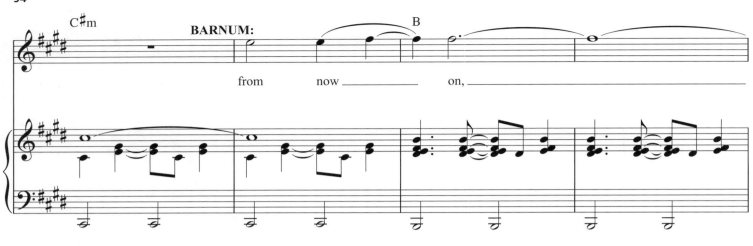

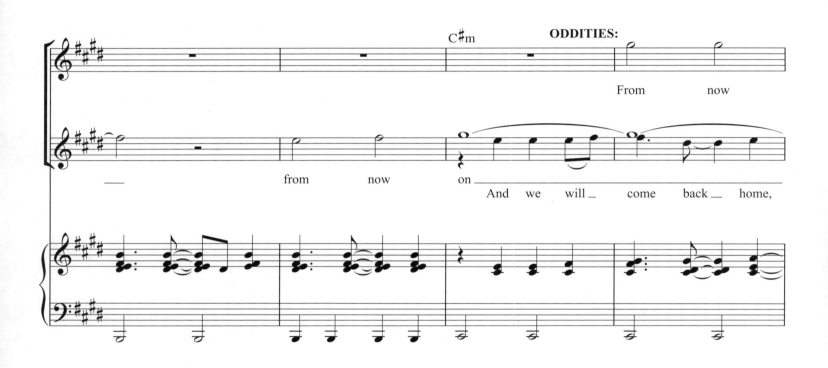

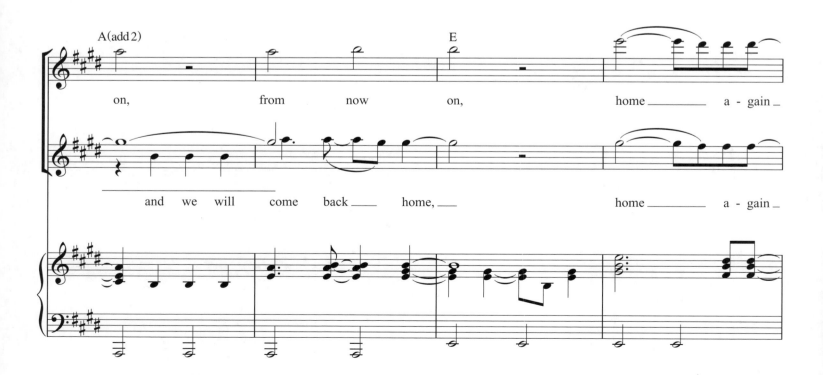

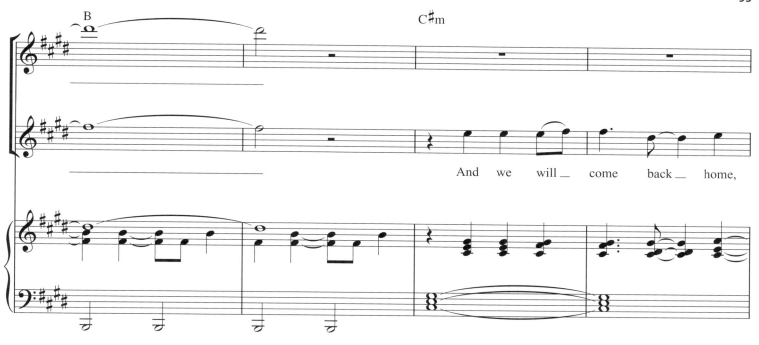